ISBN 978-0-265-97070-6
PIBN 10917401

The College Greetings

The College Greetings

The College Greetings is published monthly by the students of Illinois Woman's College.

Contributions to its pages are solicited from the students of all deparments, and from the alumnae. They are due the fifteenth of each month.

Subscriptions, $1.00 a year, payable in advance. Single copies 15c.

Entered at Jacksonville Postoffice as second class matter.

CONTENTS

(Written for the Fiftieth Anniversary by Mrs. Alice Don Carlos Vogel).

To thee, our alma mater,
    From far and near we come,
To swell with hearts and voices,
    This happy welcome home.
Thy children come o'er mountain,
    From woodland, vale and lea,
To hail with gladdest paeans,
    Thy golden Jubilee.

From far Hawaii, girt by
    Pacific waters blue,
From China and Bulgaria
    Come greeting fond and true.
And friends of auld lang syne, who
    From earthly cares are free,
In happy realms Elysian
    Smile on our Jubilee.

From chaliced cups, bright flowers
    Distil their perfumes rare,
While carols sweet of song-birds
    Fill all the sunny air.
The winds in softest cadence
    Waft greetings glad and free,
And whisper benedictions,
    On this our Jubilee.
May we from every burden
    Of sin's alluring way,
Go forth anew, unfettered,
    This joyous festal day;
As Hebrew slaves of old, were
    From thrall of bondage free,
And hailed from glad rejoicing,
    Their Fiftieth Jubliee.
        —Alice Don Carlos Vogel.

THE FOUNDERS.

In 1845 The Reverend Peter Akers drew up a memorial to the Illinois Conference asking for the establishment of an institution for the higher education of young women. Action was postponed for a year. In 1846 the Illinois Annual Conference of the Methodist Church in session at Paris, Illinois, appointed a committee with power to organize the school. This committee was appointed on September 23, and on October 10 met in Jacksonville, where they first organized and made definite plans for the new undertaking. The Rev. Peter Akers, Rev. Peter Cartwright, Rev. D. R. Trotter, Rev. William J. Rutledge, Rev. William C. Stribling, William Thomas, Matthew Stacy, Nicholas Milburn and William Brown were the first Board of Trustees, the founders of our College.

This was pioneer work, and these founders were pioneers, leaders in the new life of the young prairie state. Most of them had come from the older communities of the East and South. They were active in all the work that was being done to build our state. Our first founder Peter Akers, was a Virginian, born in Campbell Co., September 1, 1790. Admitted to the bar in Kentucky in 1817, he became converted and joined the Methodist Church in 1821 and soon began preaching. He had come to Illinois in 1832, was president of McKendree College '33-4, and then established a "Manual Labor School" near Jacksonville, maintaining it for several years. At the time when our College was founded he was presiding Elder.

The most striking figure among these first trustees was Peter Cartwright, the first President of the Board, whose activities and eccentricities have made his name a household word in Illinois. He too was a Virginian, born in Amherst County, September 1, 1785. His family came to Kentucky in 1790. At the age of sixteen he "got religion" sold his race horse and abjured dancing, gambling and swearing. Only two years later he entered the ministry. The work of those days was hard in every way. The minister must live on horseback, have no regard for heat or cold, rain or frost and ride steadily on where roads, where they existed at all, were even worse than they are now. Peter Cartwright worked for the Lord and fought the Devil and all his works. This quite literally sometimes, when the devil appeared to be incarnate in the person of some recalcitrant listener. For fifty years he was Presiding Elder. In 1828 and in 1832 he was elected to the legislature, and in 1846 was defeated for Congress by Abraham Lincoln. A man of little formal education himself, he always worked vigorously and gave richly for the cause of education. Yet he was opposed to the idea of special formal training for the ministry, arguing that its failure had been proved in other denominations. His own books are worth reading as records of stirring times and of a wonderful personality.

The first Secretary of the Board was William Brown, born in Cynthiana, Kentucky, January 1, 1810. For a time he held the chair of Political Economy and Constitutional Law at McKendree College, and a series of addresses is preserved that he delivered in the cause of education in the Hall of Representatives. He came to Jacksonville in 1833 and was an active worker in his church and in the whole community. In these early days he was living on East State st., not far from the Square.

The Treasurer elected at this first meeting was Matthew Stacy, at this time the County Judge or Probate Justice of the Peace, as they called it then. His name appears frequently on the list of city officers.

Another Virginian on the Board was The Reverend William Rutledge, born in 1820. He joined the Illinois Conference when twenty-one. For a time he was agent for the new College. In later years he was an Army Chaplain, and one of the founders of the G. A. R. His brother George, also a minister, was one of the strong friends of the struggling little College.

Among all these Virginians and Kentuckians was one man who could claim the Quaker City as his early home, Nicholas Milburn, whose family came to Jacksonville in 1838. They had come by way of the Ohio River to St. Louis, from there to Naples, and then to Jacksonville by wagon. His brother was the famous blind preacher who for a time, in spite of his blindness, rode a circuit of two hundred miles and was later Chaplain of Congress. The family home was for many years on East State street, opposite the College and students of the later seventies tell us of going over to read to the blind chaplain.

The Rev. W. D. R. Trotter was born in Glasgow, Kentucky, March 17, 1807. After two years as a midshipman in the navy he studied law, but before he was admitted to the bar he became converted and joined the church. Then he prepared to enter the ministry. In 1833 he married Maria, daughter of Peter Cartwright. One of their children was our own dear Mrs. Wilson. He died in 1880 at the pretty old home on East State St., where his daughter Mrs. Caldwell still lives.

Still another Kentuckian was Judge William Thomas, born November 22, 1802. He was admitted to the bar in 1823 and three years later came to Jacksonville, where he taught the first school in the little town. It was a "subscription school", each patron paying a fixed sum. The school house was near the southeast corner of the square and was a little log building, with a "sod and stick" chimney, three windows and slab seats.

He taught reading, writing, and the ground rules of arithmetic, coming to the school house early in the morning to build the fire. He fought in the Winnebago War in '27, and in the Black Hawk war. Judge Thomas not only taught the first school but was active in the organizing of other schools, our own among many of them. As a member of the Legislature he used his influence for the establishment of the schools for the Blind and the Deaf.

Seventy years ago! The State was still young, its admission to the Union not yet thirty years old. Its entire population was only 800,000. Railroads had hardly begun. Travel over the uncultivated prairie was slow and difficult. Judge Thomas Ford was governor of the State. In this year Abraham Lincoln was elected to Congress and Stephen A. Douglas to the Senate. The Mormon War was over and the Mormons were leaving Nauvoo on their frightful journey to the Far West. The Mexican War had begun. Duelling, never a very popular amusement in our State, was dying out in ridicule. Movements were in progress for the establishment of the great State Institutions for the education of the Deaf and Blind. Free schools—public schools, we call them now—were of few years standing and slowly increasing in number.

Jacksonville had been founded in 1825 and named for Andrew Jackson. In 1846 it is described as a pleasant little village of two thousand inhabitants. The houses were small, low and plain, and some of the prominent citizens were still living in log houses. The streets were unpaved and remained so for nearly forty years more—for the paving in Jacksonville is really not as old as some of us have thought. The Court House, the first brick building in the County, still stood in the Square, in the center of the square mile originally planned as the limit of the town. Outside of the town, on the hill to the west, stood Illinois College, founded in '29, its President at this time Julian M. Sturtevant. The Jacksonville Female Academy, opened in '33, had just begun to graduate classes. There was no organized system of public schools and the first city school house was yet to be built. Work was going on on the first building for the School for the Deaf, west of the town.

There were six churches in the little town. The two Presbyterian churches and the Baptist church were on West State St., near the Square. The Congregational church still stood on the East side of the Square. The little Episcopalian church on the present site but facing on Morgan St. is said to have had the first organ in the town. The Methodist church, east of the Square, but nearer it than the present site of Centenary, was the meeting place of the first Trustees of the College. Here they met and organized The Illinois Conference Female Academy, and here in the following Fall the first classes met the first Principal, The Rev. Nicholas Bastim.

The Square was not merely the center of the town but the center of its life. Here were not only the stores and offices, but the Court House, at least one church, and a hotel, the Morgan House. Here also was the railroad station, for the first steam railroad in the State, the "Northern Cars", then ran down State St., and through the Square. It had been built from Meredosia to Jacksonville in '39, and extended to Springfield in '41. The first train ran into Springfield in February, '42, and people boasted proudly of going from there to St. Louis in a day and a night. The one engine was called "The Pioneer", and tradition has it the train was even more inclined to lateness and irregularity than its successors over the same route now. Finally the engineer ran The Pioneer off the track east of Jacksonville, and she lay neglected, rusting in the weeds, for nearly a year, while mules drew the little train up or down State street, past the site of the new college for women. Two stage routes also started from the Square, with stages advertised to leave three times a week for Alton, and as often for Quincy. The "Underground Railway" also carried many passengers through Jacksonville, but it operated only at night and took pains not to announce its routes or times of departure publicly.

Here then, in this town, and in these days our founders met and organized the school first incorporated as The Illinois Conference Female Academy, from which our College has grown.   —Miss Johnston.

THE PRESIDENTS.

(In the following article, the accounts of Drs. McCoy and Short were contributed by Miss Dimmitt)

———

Emerson once said, "An institution can be no stronger than its head." If this is true, then the Woman's College has been peculiarly fortunate to have had for its presidents, men of courage and strength; the kind of courage that enabled them to build for present needs and future greatness, the kind of strength that permitted to obstacles to thwart their ultimate purpose. The acquisition, of property, the erection of buildings, the development of departments for special courses, the growth of the curriculum from that of a high school to college standard all point to the efforts and achievements of the seven presidents under whose guidance the school has existed. The casual visitor of today sees the several hundreds of students going about their work and play, and as he compliments the president upon the tangible result of years of planning, disapointments and hopes, how seldom does he realize that what has already been accomplished is but a stepping stone to the plans even now under way for a greater I. W. C.

It is worthy of note that the school's seventy years of history show only seven changes in administration. It was the pleasure of Dr. James G. Jacques to first occupy the presidency of the school and his seven years of service tell a story of splendid effort and devotion brought to bear upon his difficult task. At the time of the fiftieth anniversary Dr. Jacques was present, and as he was introduced to the alumnae by one who had known him long and intimately he was characterized as "our first president whose powerful personality and unselfish devotion contributed materially to the success of our college." His peculiar fitness for this position doubtless lay in the fact that he had an unusual faith in woman's place in the world and in her ability to fill that place were she properly trained. That his faith was not shattered, his own words, from his Jubilee address are adequate proof, "The early success of the institution was a matter of astonishment to many of its most sanguine and enthusiastic friends, and as success has attended the college for half a century, special mention is not required, except to say, behold these daughters and look upon these sisters! Better evidence of success achieved could not be produced, and nothing beyond this could be desired. Their credentials will bear the closest scrutiny."

In fact a vital faith in all humanity seems to have been his chief characteristic, that this faith was tempered with discernment is shown in his work with Gov. Yates. At the outbreak of the war the Governor had sent for him to come to Springfield where he became an invaluable adviser. One day a blunt, calm man obtained an interview with the Governor for the purpose of telling him he thought that he knew how to get troops for him. The governor, unimpressed by the stranger's crude manner, would have hastily dismissed him, but Jacques who was present suggested that he be asked to return on the following day. Persuaded by Jacques, Governor Yates consented to allow the stranger a desk in his office, and gave him the task of writing letters. About two weeks later the Governor said to Jacques, 'That man you thought was one I should keep, hasn't yet written a letter I'd send out."

"I didn't suppose", replied Jacques, "that he would be valuable as a clerk, I considered him better as a military drill master. Now there's the Twenty-first on the borders of mutiny. Put him in charge of them and see what's in him."

"By, George, I'll do it."

By heeding this advice of the ex school-master parson, the world knows the rest, for that was the beginning of Grant's career. Since Dr. Jacques was not the type of man to send others into danger, while he himself remained safely at home, he, too, soon joined the defenders of the flag. To this self appointed task he brought to bear the same enthusiasm, interest and spirit of helpfulness which had characterized his management of the early days of I. W. C. At the close of the war he returned to his earlier calling, that of preaching.

Those of us, who are dependent upon records for our acquaintance with Dr. Jacques, conclude that his pleasing personality, his scholarly habits and natural kindliness give him the right to the title conferred upon him by one of his students, "The Father of Our College."

So meagre are the records concerning his successor, Dr. Andrus, that we know little of his work. He occupied the office only one year. He was a man of wide experience, having had much to do with the making of the early history of Illinois Wesleyan, of McKendree College, of Chaddock at Quincy, of Asbury, which later became DePauw. In spite of his long and efficient connections with colleges he seems to have preferred the regular-work of the ministry and always eagerly returned to it whenever the opportunity presented itself.

There followed the brief and unhappy presidency of Dr. Asa McCoy, for during his first term his wife to whom he was devotedly attached, passed away.

The children of this first marriage all died and from these successive blows he never recovered. In writing to a friend in whose home he had been a guest Mr. McCoy thus movingly expressed himself—"You do not know how I envied you when I saw you with your little ones about you when my own had just found its grassy bed." So when the last and greatest of these piercing sorrows came, he resigned as president and re-entered the traveling connection of the conference, serving some years and dying only a few years ago after many years of superannuation.

For his day he was considered a thorough scholar, expressing himself with great beauty in writing, and as principal of a Young Ladies Academy located at Griggsville he had been highly successful, but he was one without the power of reaction from a blow as crushing as that dealt in the second year of his occupancy here in the old "Female College."

Dr. Adams, who followed Dr. McCoy, acted as president for ten years, and during his administration he served the school most effciently. The only available information as to his work comes from a sketch

written by Mrs. Belle Paxton Drury '63, at the time of
the Fiftieth Anniversary. He, like his predecessors,
was a member of the Methodist ministry, and his life
work was divided between teaching and preaching, In
concluding her sketch, Mrs. Drury paid him the following sincere and loving tribute. "We who are privileged to claim Charles Adams as our beloved teacher and
friend, may we not gather some inspiration from the
record of this holy and useful life, calling his God, our
God, and his Saviour our "Strength" and our "Redeem-
er."" Not only was Dr. Adams a preacher of convinc-
ing words and a teacher of real merit, but he was also
a writer of more than average merit. The following
poem was written while he was president of I. W. C.

JACKSONVILLE,

How fair the youthful city lies
    With sunny skies spread out above:
How goodly do her dwellings rise
    The homes of comfort and of love.

And see how East and South and West
    Those massive edifices tower;
Where come afflicted ones to rest
    Or wear away life's weary hour.

Such were thy gifts, great Christ, to men
    From far the weeping and distressed
Came with each varied grief and pain
    And found repose upon thy breast.

And see where learning's graceful hand
    Beckons within her sacred bowers,
Young men and maidens of the land
    To crown them with her choicest flowers.

See where the churches high uplift
  Their sacred walls to welcome thee:
The school-house, too, that other gift
  Of Virtue, Light and Liberty.

Now lift thine eyes and look beyond
  Wide o'er the landscape far and near,
Fair as the vale of Trebizand
  And fertile as the famed Cashmere.

At sundown of the century
  Oh! what a scene the eye shall fill.
Of him who in that hour shall see
  The fairy realm of Jacksonville.

In 1868 Dr. Wm. H. DeMotte came to take up the work where Dr. Adams had left it. One of his students in speaking of her first interview with him describes him in the following manner, "I was ushered into the room to meet our president, Dr. DeMotte, pictured by my youthful fancy as some one very austere and of whom I thought, as the lump in my throat grew larger, I was going to be very much afraid. But when he met us with his genial, kindly manner, these illusions were dispelled to be replaced by feelings of confidence and respect that were unchanged in all our relations of president and student." This seems to be the general opinion of all those who knew him during his term of office, for in speaking of him there is always a smile of pleasant remembrance and invariably the words "genial", "kindly" and "sympathetic" are used to characterize his every word and action. Although Dr. DeMotte served during the time, when disaster came to the school, his sturdy spirit refused to be down-cast, and what "the fire" destroyed he immediately set about to replace. As he, with characteristic optimism stated the matter, "Fire is not always an unmitigated evil. Somewhat of value was destroyed. Somewhat, also, of the worthless, even the bad burnt up. If the legitimate tenants were ousted, so also were the rats and roaches." Thus, out of an unfortunate circumstance he saw an opportunity, for growth and improvement. It was at this time that many changes of great benefit were made. Indeed the keynote of Dr. DeMotte's administration and of his helpful interest after he had left the college might be summed up in the single word, "advancement."

Of Dr. William F. Short whose presidency covered eighteen years an old student writes thus—"I was but little more than a child when I saw him first. It was on the occasion of my first formal entrance into the College and very formal, indeed, it seemed to me, then. My mother had taken my younger and smaller sister and myself over to inquire of our fitness for the Intermediate Department and I have never forgotten the gracious and courtly manner of our greeting. He was in the office and while we were sitting there Mrs. Short entered and with a smile asked, "Mr. Short, can you let me have five cents?"

As I recollect it the change was needed in the settlement of some bill she held in her hand. With a twinkle of the eye he reached the small coin over to her, remarking, "You are exceedingly modest in your demands this morning, my dear."

It was the geniality, the bright turn to his thought and the grace of him in connection with this trival incident which stamped themselves indelibly upon my memory. Others may think of him as an executive and he must have had gifts in that direction to have so long and successfully filled high offices in both church and state, but to me, he was first and last the ideal of a gentleman.

He could be withering in rebuke and terrible in judgment when in his opinion, the occasion demanded it: but there was the gentleness of a father for all who deserved it and an appreciation of honest and persistent effort which in my own case, at least, was a trumphet call stimulating every faculty. I shall never forget the evening he walked to my home—he was then the busy superintendent of the Blind—on purpose to extend his felicitations on a very small and now quite forgotten triumph which I had just achieved. The warmth of his handclasp, the beam in his eye, the pride in me, his old pupil—these were things well worth making any effort to obtain. I loved and honored him.

It is true there have been others before and since his time filling the office he so long administered and doubtless there will be many others yet to come—a long line, perhaps, of able and distinguished men. But to me there can never be another such as Dr. William F. Short, my president!

Anyone who has known the college in later years knows of the work that has been accomplished during the years that Dr. Harker has been at its head. Upon the foundations so painstakingly laid by his predecessors, he has been able to build in a manner which has far exceeded the dreams of even the most visionary. At the time of the Fiftieth Anniversary, Dr. Harker made the following statement as to the needs of the college:

1. We need the Lurton property. The College is growing and must have more room. The Lurton property adjoins the College on the west, is 175 by 580 feet, and must be added if the College continues to grow.

2. We need two society halls. The College has two as good literary societies as can be found in Illinois, the oldest women's societies in the state. They have no room to meet in.

3. We need a gymnasium. We have been doing good work in physical culture for three years past, but we have been pushed from one room to another, and need a permanent place.

4. We need additions to our library and to our physical and chemical apparatus.

5. We need some scholarships for young women who are too poor to provide for their education, but who are capable and eager for the means of study. One thousand dollars will provide a permanent scholarship for tuition, and five thousand dollars a permanent scholarship for board and tuition. Who will make such an investment?

6. We need gifts for an endowment fund.

How much of this has been accomplished and how much is about to be accomplished is easily discerned by anyone who keeps informed of the progress of I. W. C. It is gratifying to know that the sacrifices of the founders, the plans and hopes of the earlier presidents, the loyalty and enthusiasm of the student body have born fruition in the present dignified standard of the College. Those of us who have heard Dr. Harker's chapel talks can never forget his frequent repetition of, "Contentment with present attainments means retrogression." Is it not this sentiment that has prompted the work of each of those who have been at the head of I. W. C.?

CHANGES IN COURSES OF STUDY IN THE ILLINOIS WOMAN'S COLLEGE FROM ITS BEGINNING TO THE PRESENT TIME.

The Illinois Conference Female Academy
1847-1851

The School was first chartered in 1847 as the Illinois Conference Female Academy. In the first catalog after announcing the Preparatory Department, in which be taught "Reading, Writing, Spelling, Defining, Geography, English Grammar, Arithmetic, Elements of Natural Science and History, Watts on the Mind, the Construction of Maps, and Needle Work," the following statement is made: "The requisites for admission into the Academic Department, are a knowledge of English Grammar, Geography, Arithmetic and History." Then comes the following course of study:

ACADEMIC DEPARTMENT
(Including Three Years)
First Year—First Term

Latin—Anthon's First Lessons.
Natural Philosophy—Parker's.
Chemistry—Gray's.
Ancient Geography—Mitchell's.
Philosophy of Natural History—Smellie's.

Second Term.

Latin—Caesar.
Mineralogy and Geology—Hitchcock's
Botany—Woods'
Physiology—Jarvis'.

Junior Year—First Term.

Latin—Cicero.
Algebra—Davie's First Lessons.
Arithmetic Reviewed.
Domestic Economy—Miss Beecher's.

Second Term.

Latin—Virgil, Prosody.
Geometry—Davie's Legendre.
Butler's Analogy.
Parker's Aids to English Composition.

Senior Year—First Term.

Mental Philosophy—Upham's.
Astronomy—Burrett's.
Natural Theology—Paley's.
Evidences of Christianity—Alexander's.
Ancient and Modern History with Chronology.

Second Term.

Rhetoric—Newman's, Parsing.
Logic—Hedge's.
Criticism—Kames'.
Moral Science—Wayland's.
Cleveland's Compendium of English Literature.

Particular attention will be paid to Reading, Penmanship, and composition, through the entire course.

The course outlined above was called the classical Course. Students who wished to omit Latin could do so, and were enrolled in the English Course, which could be completed in two years. Classical Diplomas were conferred upon those who completed the entire course of study and sustained satisfactory examinations; English Diplomas upon those who completed the course in this department.

The above courses of study seem very curious to us of the present day. It will be noted that students began the studies of the Academic Department directly from the common branches, or the present eighth grade, and that in three years they completed the entire course, including the Latin. In the first half year of Latin, they completed Anthon's First Lessons, took

Caesar the second half year, Cicero the first half year of the second year's course, and Virgil with Prosody, the second half year of the second year's course, thus completing in two years what students now take in four.   Similar progress was made in Mathematics. Algebra was completed in a half year's study in the second year of the course; Geometry in the next half year.   The Senior Class, who would rank year for year with our Third Year Academy Students, bravely tackled such subjects as—Upham's Mental Philosophy, Paley's Natural Theology, Alexander's Evidences of Christianity, Hedge's Logic, Wayland's Moral Science, together with several other subjects, equally deep and abstruse.   In the second year they had already mastered Butler's Analogy!   Verily it would seem "that there were giants in those days" intellectually, even among the women.

II.   The Illinois Conference Female College
1851-1863.

After two years work as an academy, the charter was changed and the Institution became The Illinois Conference Female College.   In this year, 1851, a primary department was added to precede the preparatory, the courses in the preparatory remaining the same as before, and the requisites for admission into the Collegiate Department remaining the same as those for the Academic Department of the Academy as given above.   The course of study is now called the Collegiate Department, and includes four years.   It seems however, that few new subjects were added to the original course of study, but that somewhat longer time was allowed for several of the subjects.   Algebra, however, is still completed in a half year.   Geometry is now given a whole year, and Analytical Geometry is introduced with a half year for study.   As before, there is an English Course, including all the subjects except the foreign languages, which may be completed in three years.

Comparing this again with our present course of study, the graduates of the College at that time in the Classical Course had spent the same time in their course as is now spent by the graduates of our Academy, and the graduates of the English Course, the same time as our Third Academy students.

It is very likely, however, that since there were very few opportunities for even the elementary education of young women at that time, the students taking these courses of study were much older than present academy students. The college year was longer, consisting of nine and a half months, the school year opening the last of September, and continuing until nearly the middle of July, with only two and a half months vacation in the year, including part of July and the months of August and September. The statement is added that "this arrangement is thought to be best, from the fact that the young ladies may be at home during the warm and sickly season."

The above Collegiate Courses of Study were continued with very little change for many years, and to prove that the "young ladies" were thoroughly equal to it, the following statement is made in the catalog of 1853—"After five years of experiment in all the departments of a thorough Classical and English course of study, the Trustees are happy to state to the numerous friends of female education, that the success of the several classes which have pursued the prescribed course of study in the Female College has been such as fully warrants them in saying that the questions of ability and propriety are settled beyond the possibility of a doubt; and they have no hesitancy in saying, that the scholarship of the young ladies will compare favorably with the scholarship of young gentlemen in the best colleges in the country."

In 1854 an advance was made in these courses of study, by requiring a half year of Latin and a half year of Algebra before entering upon the Collegiate Courses. The study of Greek was introduced and the following most interesting statement is made:- "Conscious that to the influence of the Bible we are indebted for the high rank our country has taken in the civilized world, the Board of Instruction has made arrangements to have all those pursuing a full classical course, take daily exercise in the Scriptures in the original language; so that in the four years they may be enabled to read nearly the whole Bible in the language which our Saviour and his Apostles read and spoke, and delivered to us the oracles of Divine Truth."

It appears that this experiment with regard to Greek was continued only two years. In 1856 Greek is omitted from the curriculum.

The following list of text books in use in the College in 1856 is of great interest:-

Parker's Readers, Town's Analysis, Mitchell's Geography, Stoddard's Intellectual Arithmetic, Davie's Academical and University Arithmetics, Pinneo and Bullion's English Grammars, Willard's United States, Cutter's School and Collegiate Physiologies, Watts on the Mind, Parker's Natural Philosophy, Davie's Elementary Algebra, Loomis' Algebra, Davies' Legendres, Geometry and Trigonometry, Bridge's Conic Sections, Olmstead's Natural Philosophy, Brockleby's Memeorology, Smellie's Philosophy of Natural History, Mitchell's Ancient Geography, Wood's Botany, Dew's Ancient and Modern History, Fitche's Physical Geography, Silliman's Chemistry, Newman's Rhetoric, Burritt's Astronomy, Hitchcock's Geology, Hedge's Logic, Mansfield's Political Grammar, Upham's Natural

Philosophy, Wayland's Political Economy and Moral Science, Kames' Criticism, Alexander's Evidences, Bullion's Latin Lessons, Grammar and Reader, Cooper's Virgil, Bullion's Cicero, Anthon's Sallust, and Horace, Lincoln's Livy.

In 1857 the course of study in the Collegiate Department is again dropped to three years for the Classical Course, and two years for the English Course, and the year is now divided into three terms instead of two, as before. In the first year of the College Course, after a preparation of a half year in Latin Lessons, the student takes Anthon's Sallust the first term, thus finishing in one year texts that cover a period of three years. This course of study remains with only minor changes for several years.

III. The Illinois Female College
1863-1899.

In 1863 a new charter was obtained, and the name of the school changed to the Illinois Female College. In 1899 the name was changed to Illinois Woman's College, but the charter remained the same.

In 1863 the course of study is changed to a four year course, but the change is only seeming, because in the first year of the Collegiate Course of study a student has arithmetic, Grammar, United States History and Latin Lessons, so that in reality the course is still only a three years course, above the common branches, as before.

In 1868-9, the first year of President's DeMotte's administration— the year is again divided into two terms, but the course of study remains the same. In 1875, the first year of President Short's administration, the two term arrangement is again abandoned, and the year divided into three terms, and another year is added to the course in the Collegiate Department, thus making four years again above the common branches.

In 1888 an advance of about a half year was made, by requiring a year of Algebra and a year of Latin for entrance into the Collegiate Department, the course of study remaining four years, as before. In 1890 another change was made in the introduction of what is called a Belles Lettres Course, which enabled a student to graduate in three years, without either Mathematics or foreign languages, but the regular courses still remained—an English ~~Domestic Science~~ Course of four years, which required for entrance a year of Algebra, and a Classical Course of four years, which required for entrance a year of Algebra and a year of Latin.

In 1894 the Belles Lettres Course was dropped, and the course of study advanced by the requirement of an entire preparatory year, including Algebra, Latin, or some other foreign language, Elementary Rhetoric and Ancient History, making graduation from the College a matter of five years. This continued until 1902, when another preparatory year was added, making two preparatory years and four college years, making the entire course of study six years above the common branches, and raising the College to the rank of a Junior College. The graduates of the College at this time were prepared to enter the Junior Class of the standard colleges and universities.

The Advance to Standard College Rank, 1907.

This six year arrangement continued until 1907, when the last step was taken in the advance of the college to standard college rank. The preparatory course of study was increased to four years, and enentrance to the Collegiate Department was raised to the standard requirement of fifteen units of secondary study, a standard which has since been maintained with constantly increasing efficiency.

During all these years, from the change of charter

in 1851, by which the school was advanced from Academy to College in name, the charter had given the right to confer all the regular academic degrees. Through about forty years of its history, the graduates in the Classical Course received the degree of Mistress of Liberal Arts, M. L. A., and the graduates of the English Course received the degree of Mistress of English Literature, M. E. L. These so-called degrees were continued until 1893. The first regular college degrees were granted in 1909—the degree of Bachelor of Arts, being conferred upon Elizabeth Davis and Neva Wiley. The College has been since 1909 recognized as a standard college by the North Central Association, by the University Senate of the Methodist Episcopal Church, and by many other standardizing agencies throughout the country. Its graduates have been admitted to leading universities, and have secured Master's degrees in one year of study, thus placing the College in Class A of College lists in universities and graduate schools.

The Academy to be Eliminated.

Beginning with September 1916, the Academy will be gradually abandoned. In 1916-17 the First Academy year will not be offered, and each year thereafter at least one academy year will be dropped, so that by 1919 the Academy will be entirely eliminated.

The College also announces its definite policy to emphasize the full and regular college work, to seek quite definitely students who expect to take the full four year college course, and to limit the number entering each year, so as to give every student the best possible instruction and equipment without crowding. It will be the definite aim of the College to seek, not quantity, but quality, to provide every department with the best possible equipment, and with professors of the highest ability and efficiency.

—Dr. Joseph R. Harker.

The Buildings.

ILL. CONFERENCE FEMALE COLLEGE, 1856.

To the historian a fixed date is an object of no mean regard. It may not, perhaps, charm from him the rhapsody that choruses a poet's sweetheart but it is an object of great regard for all that. It is his point of fortunate departure, his golden peg in an otherwise baffling wall, the string to the kite of his theory, the 'Mene, mene, tekel upharson' to his detractors. What is it not? Happy are the people hinged by a fixed date unto the universal. Jacksonville, the middle west, has such a fixed date, and from it may be chronicled innumerable and significant exits and entrances in her history. Let us line it deep and large in all our annal books, this birth date of the Woman's College, and laying aside all gamesome mood, in very thankfulness for the seventy years between, walk quietly around our buildings to tell the towers thereof and to mark well her bulwarks. Not by day this time, but under the stars and hushed by the shadows of old trees—how old, I wonder, when in 1870 the old corner stone was swung into place at the northeast corner of the second main building to be erected.

With the first building, swept away by a disaster-our fire in February 1870—twenty years after its erection, we are doubtless familiar from old cuts. It was an imposing rectangle of red brick, dubbed face-tiously, the red brick mill, by the young gentlemen who sometimes called. How did they look, we wonder—those callers who trod the trim brick walk that led from the gate of the plank fence to our old front door, labelled, perhaps and perhaps not, "The Illinois Conference Female Academy?" The dignity of the old building is evident. An old catalog—1856-57 describes it; "one hundred feet in length by fifty feet in breadth, four stories high and with a basement of massive (granite) range work,—superstructure of best brick material. The front is ornamented with four massive Corinthian columns resting upon a fine cutstone portico, which is surmounted by a handsome observatory overlooking the town and vicinity." A broad hall divided the first floor. The chapel was east of this and the reception room and president's rooms were west and were differentiated from the rest of the house by carpets. Dining room and kitchens were below, recitation rooms occupied the second floor, and above all were the rooms of the girls who worked—we suppose—and played and dreamed in universal fashion. We wish the old walls and the old girls could come back this commencement not just their conjured ghosts from the shadows of the trees.

The second building seems to have sprung by miracle from the ashes of that February fire of 1870. Several changes are to be noted: no broad hall divided the main floor; instead of the high pillared porch there was an entrance to a lower vestibule, much like that we now call our old entrance; the cupola was no more. Never again would the small children of dignified presidents enjoy the delectable slide from the window in this cupola to the roof of the high porch—once theirs by divine right. Tho different this building was as dignified and as enterprising a structure as the first and a fit embodiment of the simple dignity, the heroic devotion of the founders of the college, men of the fifties and men of the seventies who worked and sacrificed more than we shall ever know. The work of '47-'50 was pioneer work; the work of the seventies was in the face of great odds and under heavy burden.

But how did the building look? Then as now high and solemn windows flanked the front door, five to the east, four to the west, duplicated below and above. At the northeast corner, just above the corner stone with its legend of the first fixed date in the history, respectfully announced in our first paragraph,—three windows looked out from the library and president's class room combined. The two to the west of them belonged to the spacious dignity,—I should say dignified spaciousness if truth permitted, of the president's office. Later this became the library annex; later still an English office. Now it has changed flags altogether and abides among us as the "petit salon" of the French department.

Under the corner room, from the rebuilding of '70 way down to the installation of the present heating plant in 1904, a furnace puffed and steamed. It was a great thing in its day. No more stoves to tend, dozens of them; no more wood to carry up long and creaking stairs; no more joys of winter getting one up in the small cold hours of the morning to start the fire. It was surely a great thing but better systems were devised and the old furnace came to be but a necessary evil at best. What a noise it made and how hot those library floors used to get!

Fewer changes marked the west half of the old building. The reception room has known many refurnishings, but has never relinquished its dignified posi tion. For many years the third floor above, was also one big room, the art studio. When this finally moved into the Lurton house, the big room become gymnasium and elocution room combined. Below it for nearly forty years were the rooms of the lady principal, forerunner to the college dean. From her fine west windows she could look down in early days upon a little gallery, often "lady-laden", that ran across the front of the wing added in 1854 to the south west corner of the main building. Later the gallery was replaced by a broad porch upon which opened the central hall of the wing. The outside entrance to the dining room, moved here when the wing was added, was below the porch and from it streamed the girls after meal time in friendly groups or in long lines duly hatted and chaperoned for the morning constitutional around the block. At the northwest and some what shielded by the Lurton house lay croquet grounds much heralded as a resort becoming the dignity of young ladies and the religion of Methodists.

East State street was very desirable in the early days, a sort of quality row and eloquent as it has always been of the life of the college. Up and down this old thoroughfare pass all our friends and up and down it have travelled all our daughters in their comings and their goings, on foot, in hack, or street car. Now they often arrive in easy comfort of automobile; years ago they sometimes came by heavy wagon with a little trunk and perhaps a feather bed roped in behind the high seat where a girl and her father sat rather silent as became an auspicious occasion. If arriving from the east, they passed the homes of the Mathers, John and Wesley, of Preston Spales and of Abner Yates. Across the street lived Mr. Richard Yates, Illinois War Governor. To the west of the Yates homestead were two small frame houses, one story and each with two low front doors, the Milburn house and the Trotter house. Further west was the old Price home and on the south side of the street lived the Lurtons, the Blacks and the Willards,—fine old families and our good friends. South, but separated by a reach of vegetable garden and fragrant current bushes, lived Mr. Geo. Rutledge.

The medieval history of institutions as of men, seldom has the same absorbing interest tendered the period of beginnings. But an even greater impulsion than this fact hurries the writer of this paper straight into modern history when she quits the early building activities. A little diagram hanging in President Harker's office tells the story. The next date after the rebuilding of '72 following the third fire, is '99! For twenty-five years no sound of plane or hammer! The old quarters sufficed. Then came the lengthening of the southeast wing to enlarge the chapel and provide further recitation rooms. This necessitated the removal of the stage and the stained glass windows at the south end of the old chapel. The College Greetings of September 1899, describing the addition remarks that back of the recitation rooms "a graceful staircase leads to the hall above where are the new bath rooms.—The additional space in the basement gives the college two new laboratories and a gymnasium." Many more changes came the following year in the extension of the dining room wing; and especially in 1902 in the erection of the west end of the present main building. What excitement there was when the old wing porch was torn away and the first plows cut deep black furrows in the smooth lawn under our windows those hot spring days! And how eagerly some of us went over the plans and then dreamed about them all the summer following! There were laboratories in the basement. The offices, an Art Studio, Mrs. Harker's parlors and two society rooms— the present library—on the third floor. We rejoiced especially in our broader central stairs and in the spaciousness of the front hall. The second floor was all dormitory, and the third added much to the accomodations of the music department, heretofore confined to the third floor of the west wing.

Nineteen-four saw the erection of the laundry and power house and the removal of the old furnaces to safer as well as larger quarters.

All sorts of extremities of labor and problems grave and gay marked the building of Music Hall. The summer was hot, materials were sometimes delayed and strikes threatened and even came to pass. It was a joy delayed,—perhaps all the greater when it came. Many who read this will remember the finishing touches and the opening days. All the special departments awaited its hospitable summons to a local habitation if not a name. The Domestic Science Department rejoiced in the fine basement rooms, and the Art was jubilant at the top of the house. Music reigned between and celebrated its installation with a fine concert. All the town came to look and to listen.

One more building remains for my chronicle. Many are to come but I am only annalist of the past not prophet of the future. The great strides of the college seems to be marked by a succession of front doors gradually moving to the left. Harker Hall takes us around the corner. There's no telling where the next will be. Describe Harker Hall? That is difficult. Most of us know it so well, its great battlemented rectangle of red brick; its broad north and south corri-

dors, its class rooms and laboratories to right and to left on the first two floors,—its three floors of students' rooms.   Details of form and furnishing must be crowded out. Two points of significant suggestion must be noted in closing:—the radiant gleam of a wireless apparatus way up on top, symbolic of we know not what lines of far and fine connection in the heavens; and a lovely brass tablet dated 1909 in the first floor corridor, naming the hall in recognition of the devotion and the service of the beloved president of the college, Dr. Harker.   —Miss Neville

IN SOCIAL CONTACT.

In all the discipline of a College experience the value of that which comes from residence in the community life of the small college must not be overlooked.

From the small group of her home circle the girl entering College keenly feels the changed proportion in her relationship to the larger group surrounding her

In her own room, in the corridors and dining hall, and on the campus there is an intimate contact with teachers and fellow students, yet she misses an accustomed freedom. In the new conventions to be observed she after awhile comes to realize that the new rules of conduct are not arbitrary, but they protect the comfort and right of the many, rather than grant privilege to the few. And in this miniature democracy she learns that the grace of adaptibility, consideration and courtesyesy is essential in a College girl as is the ability to solve mathematical problems or translate orations.

Through all the passing years of Illinois Woman's College there has developed a valued tradition that young ladies going out from her walls bear with them a womanly grace and sincerity of purpose characteristic of the atmosphere and influence of their Alma Mater.

There is a fascinating interest in the stories which alumnae of early years relate when they are with us on reunion occasions. We do not want to forget how the opening days of the College in 1848-49 and the fifties brought the students. In carriages and wagons, from places far and near, they came with their hair covered trunks, their boxes of home made candles, their pretty poke bonnets in band boxes, and perhaps a feather bed, if a fond mother wished her daughter to have the accustomed comfort. Until the completion of the first College building, with its stately columns reaching to the top of the third story, board was secured among the people of the town. But for many years, whether living in the college dormitory or elsewhere, there were apt to be three or four girls in a room, and a little stove with wood for fuel was the commanding object on one side of it. A girl leaving the room on any errand was apt to be followed by calls from her room-mate to "bring some wood up when you come back." A strip of molding with hooks or nails answered in place of a closet and held the modest wardrobes deemed suitable for school girl use. There were no bath rooms or running water anywhere, and some of the students provided themselves with wooden wash tubs, which, when not in use, could be pushed under the bed, with the various devices used with it to provide a temporary privacy. It is hard to conceive what disorder the daily morning inspection would have revealed had it not been for the stow-away place under the bed, concealed by the valence surrounding at least two sides of it.

Gathered about the little table in the evening study hours the girls labored over their compositions, or mastered the problems in Loomis' Algebra in a way which we still hear "made things hum" in that remarkable class room. Room-mates took turns in furnishing a dozen candles which were burned one at a time, unless some especially dark and dismal task called for more light. Then they indulged themselves with a brilliant illumination and recklessly burned two or three.

The play side of a young girl's life sixty and seventy years ago was given little thought after she had outgrown her doll. She was then supposed to be a lady, and such was her constant admonition. Athletic impulses were disgraceful and hoyden—to be suppressed at all times. Calisthenics with wands and dumbbells were practiced as conducive to grace. But there were few games and little play. A daily walk and sometimes a chance to get several girls in a recitation room large enough to play "Poor pussy wants a corner" was nearly all the fun that was offered. About 1860 a pretty and popular lawn game, called Grace-hoops, was introduced. The hoops were smoothly wound with colored ribbons and with polished sticks, they were thrown from one to another in the group or circle playing the game. If by chance a hoop fell encircling the head of a player, a forfeit was paid. Young ladies in their white dresses with slippers scarcely peeping beneath the full hooped skirts, with their ribbon sashes of pink and blue, made a charming picture on the lawn in this graceful exercise. Croquet and archery came in later, alternating in popularity. And these have been followed by the basket ball, tennis, hockey, and golf of popularity in recent years.

For indoors, there was a time when tableaux and charades were the ruling passion. A huge dining table, stored in a school room, furnished the stage for these picture shows. Many were the closets and attics ransacked to furnish costumes for the wedding scenes and the historic tragedies there enacted.

The Belles Lettres and Phi Nu societies in their open meetings and exhibitions never failed to overcrowd the chapel, and the occasional concerts given by Mrs. Rapelje and her successors were events of community interest. Friends of the faculty and students were invited to remain after the program until the warning bell sounded good-night.

But the real social feature of the earliest years were an annual picnic in the spring and a mid-winter reception, or President's levee, as it was called. These were occasions of great preparation, calling for new gowns and ribbons. The students, as well as the officers of the College, suggested the names of guests, and every lassie had her escort when the picnic collation was spread, or when the banquet in the dining hall was served. Every kind of meat and cake that could be secured was provided and the company included the professional and business men of the community, as well as the students of the schools. The picnics were held at the end of East State street, sometimes in Father Stribbling's pasture, extending to the woods of what is now the Lurton farm, and at other times on the North side of the street in the Grierson pasture, where stately trees and a band stand in well kept grounds were recognized attractions. Young Ben Grierson here drilled the membres of his band, a company that is still recalled with appreciation by some of the young-hearted gray beards of Jacksonville. With his love of music, Ben Grierson also had a fine gift of command and leadership which brought him into prominence during the Civil War, and made his name as General Grierson permanent in the history of our country.

Visits to the State Schools for the deaf and for the blind, to the hospital for the insane and to the Morgan County Alms House were regular events in the school year for a long period. They still attract the interest of many students, who use the weekly holiday for these excursions.

In all times the years of learning have been the years of romance. The beautiful flower of youth so ordains it. No wonder that the convent system of seclusion, mistrust and espionage brought forth its natural fruits. Clandestine breaking of rules and regulations had their episodes in midnight feasts with curtained transoms, often followed by the panic of discovery.

In the College, as well as without, barriers that forbade a frank and well regulated social contact could not prevent the stolen glance, the serenade and sometimes the secret tryst. The story of such foolish adventure, with the tragic reprimand that followed, has been handed down through many succeding generations of students and always elicits the interest of sympathetic Romeos and Juliets.

Educators have not yet solved the problem of a sane and well-balanced proportion between study and recreation. But the consideration being given the subject, promises that the future solution must be such as will deveolp higher standards that will influence and make better the human relationships in all the ways of life.

In the Woman's College which was founded by the generosity and sacrifice of many donors it was to be expected that the students would pass on to others something of the benefit that they received. During the Civil War this was done by Louise Vance, as she went into the hospital camps, where she spent almost three years nursing the sick and wounded soldiers, part of that time being associated with Mrs. Bickerdike. Later, the Woman's Foreign Missionary Society, with its touching appeals, prompted the support of orphans and Bible women in India, Japan and China, and called several of our alumnae to the work in those fields. The Y. W. C. A. has still further broadened the outlook and has led to the sending of Christmas boxes of dressed dolls to various settlement houses in Chicago, to the carrying of Thanksgiving baskets to deserving families in Jacksonville, the names being sent to the College by the Associated Charities, or by physicians of the city. The singing of Christmas Carols at the homes of the aged and shut-in people, who are pleased to receive such courtesy, has for ten or twelve years been a college custom on the evening before holiday vacation.

The most recent development in this beautiful impulse of helpfulness is the Social Service Circle, which was organized in the fall of 1914. The Christmas tree party to the Free Kindergarten children, the contribution of gloves, stockings and blankets to the Open Air School for Tubercular children, the sewing, cooking and gymnasium classes for the maids employed in the College, are only a part of the things initiated and carried out by this circle.

The course of study followed along these lines of service, and the well directed impulse, will send every young woman back to her community a valuable coworker in all that will lift and benefit its standard of life.　　　　　　　—Mrs. Belle Short Lambert.

The College Greetings

Vol. XX.   Jacksonville, Ill., May, 1916.   No. 8

Committe for Anniversary Number—Chairman, Janette C.
    Powell, Miss Jennie Anderson, Miss Lois Coultas, Miss
    Dorothea Washburne.
Faculty Adviser—Miss Jennie Anderson.
Editor-in-chief—Ruth Want.
Associate and Alumnae Editor—Alma Harmel.
Assistant Editors—Norma Perbix, Margaret Slatten.
Art Editor—Ruth Patton.
Business Manager—Ruth Taylor.
Assistant Business Managers—Phyllis Wilkinson, Audra Miller.

Editorial

Several years ago a weary editor laid aside the editorial pen and turned the key of the Greetings office, with what, she sternly told herself was a sigh of relief.If she had been perfectly truthful, however, she would have admitted that the relief was tempered with a certain amount of regret, for in spite of the trials and embarrassments incident to the issuing of the "Greetings," there had been numerous compensations. Now that the unexpected opportunity of again turning the key and dipping the pen into the waiting ink has presented itself, the pleasure of returning to old duties has been very real indeed. The kindly interest of the other members of the "Anniversary committee," the efficient responses of those asked to contribute, and the ready helpfulness of the Greetings staff, have made the task an easy one. To each one who has had a share in the making of this number, and to each one who has given a cheering word of encouragement, the editor wishes to take this opportunity to say a most grateful "thank you".

In the life of an individual, the arrival of the seventieth anniversary is a time for congratulations and reminiscences, and in the life of an institution the occasion is much the same. Seventy years of history must needs be concerned with numerous stories of hopes and plans, accomplishments and disappointments. Of these latter, I. W. C. seems to have had few, just enough, perhaps, to keep her from being unpleasantly complacent and self-satisfied. Progress along many lines are proof that those interested in the school's welfare have not wrongly placed their interest. The committee for the "Anniversary number" of the "Greetings" has tried to trace the development along its various lines of growth. When the tale is finished, there comes, of course, the inevitable question of healthy activity, "What next?" The news of a few days ago answers the question in part, for "next" comes one of the long felt needs of the college, a new gymnasium.

For the last twenty years there has not been a commencement time that a plea for such a building has not been made, there has not been a campaign for funds, endowment or building, in which this lack has not been pictured. At last the plans can step from the blue prints of the architect's office to the reality of brick and mortor on the campus. Glad as we are that the "vision" can finally become an actuality, the latest official mesage should give us even greater pleasure. It is a message some of us have waited long to hear, and we hail its coming as a promise of more vital import, more far reaching effect than the erection of a dozen more dormitories might give. No longer will the effort to enlarge the attendance take precedence over all other efforts, for begining with September, 1916 the attendance will be limited. The energy thus expended will be directed into new channels and instead of the question of "How many," will be the question of "How good?"

With pride, visitors have been told to look at this new building or that new wing that meant the housing of more girls; with pride too, the growing endowment fund has been pointed to as proof of the college's many friends. Both the acquistion and the pride were legitimate, they were necessary phases of growth. Now, however, with adequate buildings, with security in the form of endowment, has come the time when the less tangible, but no less important needs can be given more attention. True scholarliness, sincerity, both of purpose and of effort, a loyalty that need never suffer disillusionment, these are the things that can not be pointed out to the visitor, but they are the things that mean much to the student, not only during her four years pursuit of her A. B., but for the after years when she measures life experiences by the theories of college days.

By the present achievements we conclude that the seventy years of history have surely fulfilled the founders' dream and the promise for the future would seem quite as worth while, as has the fulfillment of the past.

GAY DAYS

The lady of the Calendar, realizing that college to be a place of development must not be made up of work days alone, has scattered throughout the I. W. C. year a number of special days, unbirthday presents to the girls. The sage little lady has seen to it, also, that these extra events be of a widely different nature. About fifteen years ago she whispered lightly into the ears of Dr. and Mrs. Pitner, and the result of her whisper was that not in our 1916 Greetings alone we find mention of the Pitner picnic, but far back in the 1903 Greetings, we read, "Another one of those annual delights of the I. W. C. girl has come and gone. On Monday, Oct. 17, Dr. and Mrs. Pitner, well known and loved by all the college girls, entertained the faculty and students at their beautiful home, Fairview." To all at I. W. C. this is a day of autumn flowers, dry fallen leaves, long country vistas, fresh air, and of a generously given hospitality.

The lady of the Calendar moves events up, and we come to Founder's Day, which we owe to our president, Dr. Harker. To those of the last few years it may come with somewhat of a surprise that Founder's Day has been observed only since 1909. On November 5, of that year occurred the first celebration of Founders' Day. On that day Dr. William DeMotte, the fifth president of the college, gave a short address on "Some Things in the Past and a Parable for the Future," and Dr. Dan Brummitt talked on "The Call of the Twentieth Century for an educated Womanhood. President James from Illinois, Bishop McDowell, Rev. Sheridan, Richard Yates, and Senator Sherman have been with us on these days. The history of the Woman's College has been a varied one, and had it not been for these early founders, whose memory has been kept fresh in our minds the last few years, that history would have been a short one. The spirit of gratitude and the joy in giving honor to the early builders speaks much for the ideals of a college that, looking into the future, is still mindful of its past.

Following close upon Founder's Day comes Thanksgiving, a day of thankfulness for our blessings, to be sure, but also one of the brightest days in I. W. C. social life. A number of years ago, before the college had grown too big, the girls, early in the morning, put on aprons and caps, helped with the breakfast dishes, pared potatoes, washed lettuce and celery, and in other ways helped to give the maids a short rest. As the college grew, however, this plan had to be given up, for the I. W. C. girl on Thanksgiving Day is in her seat at church by half past ten. Corridor breakfasts are now served, and the dining room decoration is in the hands of the Freshman class. Candles, flowers, ferns, and interested smiling faces make the big dining room a very gay place, when the girls and the guests of the college fill it for the banquet and the toasts that are the chief event of the day. In the evening after the first excitement is over and yet before the holiday spirit has had full vent, a short surprise programme is given in the old chapel. This surprise varies from the minstrel show by Mallory Bros. to a mock or serious program given by students or faculty, and ends with the invitation from Dr. and Mrs. Harker for the students to assemble in one of the halls for hot chocolate and cakes or apples and cookies or something equally delightful.

Upon the return to the college after holiday, quiet and hard work is the order of the day until the kind social guardian again puts her hand to the helm. And this time what scurrying about for silk lined coats, what numberless trips to Woolworths for lace and buckles ensue. George Washington's birthday has once more come around, and in place of college girls, handsome Georges and winsome Marthas walk, and strut about in gorgeous raiment. Not only is this party a place for powder and patches and puffs, but a testing ground for the college girl's ingenuity and for her clever fingers. To produce a costume out of noth-

ing? Impossible! And yet it is possible, as many a
girl has proven, and as many a costume has borne wit-
ness. After the dinner comes the promenade up and
down the halls, while guests and friends look on, and
then last the entertainment. The Kisses of Marjorie,
a bright little play, has been given several times for
Washington Party night, songs, readings, pantomimes,
and tableaus have all given pleasure, too on this day.

Before the time of the spring vacation, which has
been given for the last four years, the Monday night
following Easter was known as the night of the Easter
reception. This, the most formal event of the year,
and the cause of much palpitation of the heart, at the
thought of "going down" the receiving line for the
timid one, was the time of the year when the very pret-
tiest of pretty frocks were brought out of their boxes
and donned, and questions of clothes and exact social
usage were most rife. "Excellent training for the girls
and very good for them, since they are so excited about
it", said the dean as she answered the one hundred and
oneth question on perhaps the correct way to shake
hands or on whether or not a hint should be dropped
that the man from home might not forget his dress
suit. "What a nice thing for the girls, as it gives them
something so different to do," said the Faculty, as the
girls went past chattering busily. "How perfectly delightful" came from the girl who revelled in the social
whirl and "I suppose it is good for me, but I am scared
to death", from the girl to whom such events were not
the usual thing.

After the Easter reception, longed for and eagerly
awaited, or dreaded but successfully survived, had been
passed, came May Day with its practice, and its sacrifices in time, with its hot elections and political skir-
mishing, yet with all its pleasure and its beauty. Although May Day for the last few years has been simp-

ler, groans were once heard on every hand, preparatory to the final day, when if it did not rain, the Queen would be crowned, the May Poles wound and the Grand March take place. Yet however lazy the girl beforehand, however unwilling at times her practice, when the day of days came, the eyes of the willing and the unwilling were all equally bright and satisfied with the result and with the amount of work necessary to make the day a success. May Day has seen many internal changes, but the outward seeming has of necessity been much the same. In 1906 we read of the crowning of Miss Weaver, the Lady Principal, as Queen of the May. On that day besides the crowning of the May Queen, the different classes gave stunts, sang class songs and gave class yells. One class planted an elm and a flowering bush, another presented a willow rustic seat to the college, and another had ready a big bowl of frappe for the students. In 1908 Miss Helen Colean, the first May Queen, chosen from the girls, was crowned Queen of the May. Until the last year popular election has decided the girl to whom this honor shall fall .Now from the Junior and Senior classes twelve girls are chosen by vote of the student body, and the final decision is made by lot on May Day.

The Lady of the Calendar, after having seen May Day to its close, smiled at the last jollities of its campus supper, resigns her staff to the Commencement Committee, and bides her time till the opening of a new school year.

THE COLLEGE GREETINGS.

For twenty years "The Greetings" has been the reflector of the comings and goings of our college life. What a good time the many contributors to this Anniversary Number, have had in taking down the long, slim volumes that represent the first years of existence for the College paper, and turning the pages in search of data on the "genesis and progress" of the various college organizations. The only trouble has been in staying with the subject we started out to find, for with every useful reference there has always been some other alluring headline which was only the signal for a prolonged period of digression! Not only the literary contributors but the cuts were a source of delight. For, what with the changing styles of costumes and coiffure, it has been no small diversion to trace some of our faculty through various stages of metamorphosis, beginning with their introduction as new members of the teaching staff and continuing to the present time!

Most of you know, of course, that The Greetings first began in 1896 when Dr. Harker was preparing the Alumnae for the great home gathering on the occasion of the fiftieth commencement of our Alma Mater. With the President as General Manager and Mrs. Martha Capps Oliver as Editor, the first four-paged "Jubilee Greetings" was printed. It was full of news about members of the various classes, with letters from the secretaries, and containing, too, many items about the present college. Every Alumna whose address was to be had, received one of each of the three issues that appeared and found this method of keeping in touch with college friends, highly delightful. When the great anniversary was come and gone there were many petitions for the continuance of the little news-letter. So the "College Greetings" of Illinois Female College came to be.

Literary contributors from Alumnae and from present students soon became a regular part of the paper, and the size was increased to from eight to twelve pages.   After the first twelve issues, Miss Della Dimmitt, an alumna, assumed the responsibility of Editor and put out a paper that grew steadily better under the six years of her administration.   Then ambitious students began to look wistfully toward the office.   In 1904-'5, the Senior class was granted the qrivilege of undertaking The Greetings and with Linnie E. Dowell as editor and Lena Yarnell and Golden Berryman as business managers, they set about to do it. This was Miss Neville's class of '05 of whom we have all heard so much. Alice Wadsworth, Susan Rebhan, Anne Marshall, Nell Taylor and many other girls, who are still well known in the college halls, represent those who reinforced this first student editor.   It is easy to see they were well fitted to assume such a responsibility and the paper which came from the management proves that the confidence in student ability shown by Dr. Harker and the alumnae, was not misplaced.   In fact the students were so enthusiastic over their part in the college paper that the pendulum swung to a far extreme.   Whereas the last number under the alumnae management was two-thirds news-notes about the former students with only cursory mention of present activities, the first number under the '05ers presents a decided change.   In a short note on the last page the editor explains that owing to lack of space it seems necessary to omit the alumnae notes. which will accordingly appear in the next issue!   And the same omission has been occurring frequently ever since.   Recently, there has been another reason for it—lack of material—and we wonder if the pens of the alumnae contributors are not growing rusty from disuse.   Perhaps next year we can return to a happy balance and have in our paper full representation for all daughters of the college whether they be on the hither side or the yon side of the A. B.

After the class of '05, the seniors of each succeeding year undertook the Greetings, until in 1909, a change was made to a staff composed of representatives from the various college classes. Three years later a room on the second floor Harker was given to the Greetings for an office and was furnished by the staff of that year and their adviser Miss Cowgill, with the adequate fittings which still make the office a pleasant place for work.

It is pleasant to sit at the official desk and read over the products of editors gone, to come to know——and——and——and the others who have followed in their wake, by the stamp of their personalities as recorded there. It heartens one to read of the dreams of editors past and see how they harmonize with the efforts of editors present for the College Greetings as it is to be. More pages and more and better literary contributions to fill them; more voluntary contributions; short stories; more active and significant departments, less provincialism and more awakeness to the events of the wider realm; more word and more subscriptions from the Alumnae! These are the ideals to which the editors of the future fall heir. And we wish for them speedy realization. Meanwhile, at this time of counting years and making much of birthdays, The Greetings celebrates a birthday of her own—one that marks twenty years of constant progress and seems a fitting time for making a resume of "the days that are gone" for the sake of "the days that are coming before."

— Ruth Want

STUDENTS' ASSOCIATION

On March 5, 1913, the first steps toward student government were taken. Dr. Harker then organized the College Council, made up of the heads of the college organizations and classes with the class advisers, and gave it jurisdiction over all general student activities. This was done with the purpose of unifying student life and promoting college spirit and loyalty.

During the next year, a temporary form of House Government was instituted with the permission and co-operation of the faculty. The house students assumed responsibility for their conduct within and without the dormitory and organized by the election of a Board of Proctors, as an executive body, which had a representative from each corridor and a Senior Proctor as chairman.

The College Council proved itself so worthy of the trust reposed in it by the President and Faculty and the house students shouldered with such enthusiasm their responsibilities in partial self-government that the student body was honored by a still larger gift. Believing that better organization would more effectually "unify all college activities, promote college spirit, conserve college loyalty and enthusiasm, and stand for the highest ideals of honor and true womanliness", President Harker, in behalf of the Trustees and Faculty, granted a charter to the Students' Association on October 30th, 1914, a great day in a series of years full of great days. By the middle of November the constitution of this Association had been drawn up and adopted, officers had been elected, and full fledged student government was inaugurated at Illinois Woman's College.

The legislative power is of course vested in the student body as a whole, while the executive power is placed in the hands of an executive committee made up of the major officers of the association, one member each from the Sophomore, Freshman and College Special classes, the two house-chairmen, and the Academy Proctor. The President and Vice-president of the Students' Association are elected from the coming Senior class, and the Secretary and Treasurer are elected from the in-coming Junior class. There is also a joint committee of conference that is made up of the Faculty Committee on Student Relations, and the Student officers. The Board of Proctors is the executive body for House Government. Each corridor has a representative, whose duty it is to preserve order on her corridor, to enforce all regulations in the college, and to report all irregularities. The President of the Students' Association is also chairman of this board and she and the two house chairmen constitute an inner cabinet in cases where there is no time to await the action of the Proctor Board.

We have now lived under such government for about two years. The constitution drawn up with great thought and care, has stood the test of usage wonderfully well; the house regulations, having evolved by a method similar to the infant's trial and error method, have proved satisfactory in providing for a well regulated household; but the novelty of self-government has worn off and the strength of purpose of each student is being tried. When we grow discouraged because conditions are so far below the ideal, when the realization comes so repeatedly that we are not big enough to properly meet our responsibilities, when we grow heartsick because co-operation at times dissolves into ineffective individual action, then we long to be irresponsible children again. When we see the growth of character in the Woman's College girls that shows itself in increased consideration of others, and both greater self-reliance and sympathetic understanding, and when we have the pleasant feeling of "all-togetherness" that expresses itself in true college loyalty instead of small group interest, then we are glad that we have the opportunity to be college women. We thank our Alma Mater for having given us this opportunity.   —Helen McGhee.

A HISTORY OF THE SOCIETIES.

The history of the two oldest societies—Phi Nu and Belles Lettres—is so similar, the time of their inception, their object and activities, having been almost identical, that except in the matter of those points which are of necessity individual, theirs may be treated as a joint history.

Just two years after the establishment of the "Illinois Conference Female College", Belle Lettres was founded (1851) at the instigation of Miss Sheldon, a member of the faculty. There were thirteen charter members, of whom the officers were; Margaret Morrison (Mrs. Turley), Minerva Dunlap (Mrs. Scott), Sophie Naylor (Mrs. Grubb), Melinda Harrison (Mrs. Johnson), and Alice McElroy (Mrs. Griffith of Springfield) the only surviving charter member whose reminiscences we were privileged to hear when she visited us on Founders' Day of this year.

The society was formed primarily to cultivate the literary taste of its members, though an even greater ambition was indicated by its motto: "Hic vitae activae preperamus,"   "Here we prepare for active life." Unfortunately, the fire of 1861 destroyed not only its furniture and books, but also the records of its proceedings. Little is known, therefore, of its activities before that date, but we can derive something of their nature from a program of the first Belles Lettres Exhibition (corresponding to the open meeting of today). We find this program in an old Greetings "which reported an address given before the society by Mrs. Griffith, in 1899. It reads as follows:

Illinois Conference Female College
Jacksonville
February 17, 1852
Order of Exercises
Prayer

The General Diffusion of Knowledge—Essay.
Hail Columbia, varied.
Soliloquy of a blackboard—Essay.
Ingleside—Trio.
Imagining—Essay.
Fantasia—"Low Back'd Car."
Louis Napoleon—Essay.
California Gold Hunters.
Onward and Upward—Essay.
Good-night—Song.
It will be said of us, they were in a hurry—Essay.
Scots wha hae, varied.
The Soul—a poem (original).
Praise the Lord.
Benediction.

This ambitious program was (according to Mrs. Griffith) the result of a spirit of rivalry that had grown up between Belles Lettres and Sigma Pi and Phi Alpha the literary societies at Illinois College. The learned brothers had talked so constantly and enthusiastically about their societies' lively proceedings that Belles Lettres determined to make their organization quite as vital.

Belles Lettres gave frequent "Exhibitions" and held weekly meetings. Every other week its program consisted of a debate on some current political or social question, or question of ethics (abolition, for a number of years was the absorbing topic)—the intervening week being given to a musical and literary program. The meetings were held on Tuesdays at four, a custom which, but for a fifteen minute change, has persisted to this day. Great stress was always laid on the use of the library, which was accumulated with fair rapidity, and the officers (president, vice-president, treasurer, two secretaries, critic, chaplain, sergeant-at-arms, two pages) included a librarian.

The original Belles Lettres badge consisted of two white ribbons, upon which the societies motto was printed, but was changed later to the immediate predecessor of the present pin, resembling it in outline but considerably larger in size and bearing on its surface a more complicated design. The society color was originally a light blue, but at some undiscoverable date was changed to yellow.

According to one report, Belles Lettres, for a short time previous to 1892 ceased to exist, but was in that year reorganized and has continued in its successful career ever since. Its song was written in 1898 by the present Mrs. Charles Don Carlos Vogle. In 1904 "The Belles Lettres Echo" (which no longer exists) put in its appearance, containing in its colums a journalistic summary of war news and local news, jokes and a weather forecast.

The early records, written in a script so gorgeously embellished as to put our modern chirography to shame, contain the roll of membership, followed by rows of a's, b's and c's, which represent the critic's estimate of each member's literary performance. It seems that at the end of every year the society held formal (and moist!)) Valedictory exercises, at which diplomas were presented to the members graduating from it. (To be Valedictorian was the pinnacle of social ambition. There is not, however, for all the elaborate grading system, a record of any members ever failing to graduate!

*　　*　　*　　*　　*　*　　*　　*

On December 8, 1853, the need being felt for another literary society, Phi Nu was founded. The older society drubbed them, in affectionate superiority, "The Trundle Beds" and received in return the name of "The Fossils."

Its charter members are hard to trace, but of their number we are certain of the following: Miss Johanna Wahl, President (succeeded in 1854 by Mrs. Mary Mans Smith—who was not, however, a charter member), Mrs. Elvira Hamilton Adams, Martha Maria Spaulding, (daughter of Rev. Horace Spaulding, teacher of Greek and Latin), Mrs. Caroline Potter Lacey, and Mrs. Susan Brown Bartlett.

As with its sister society the Phi Nu records of its earliest history were destroyed in the fire of 1861—at which time also it too lost its furniture and the beginnings of a library. But in 1861 it was reorganized with twenty-nine members and the encouragement of a nucleus for a new library. Many friends came to the rescue, and Sigma Pi presented the society with twenty-six volumes.

The motto chosen was "Lucem colligentes ut emittamus," "Gathering, that we may scatter light," and its modest purpose was expressed as follows: "To cultivate a correct style of composition, improve our literary taste, and mould a perfect social and moral character." It may be a sign of youth to hitch a wagon to a star, but it is also a sign of aspiration, and aspiration in these societies does seem to have proved the forerunner of achievement.

During its history Phi Nu has had either a number of journals or a journal with a number of names. At first we hear of "Wayside Gleanings", then of the "Phi Nu Gem", which name was changed in 1874 to the "Non Pareil", and later by a more diffident generation to "The Amateur." After that it was simply the Phi

Nu Bulletin" which was issued for the last time in 1913.

The constitution and by-laws were revised and amended in 1869-70 and music and oration added to the weekly programs. The offices of chorister, critic, teller, and chaplain were added to the usual offices provided for by the constitution, and the time of meeting was changed from Wednesday at three to Thursdays at four-fifteen. Later, however, it was changed to Tuesdays at four-fifteen at which time it meets today. The papers read at the meetings were graded, and as with Belles Lettres and occassionally in connection with it, Valedictory exercises were held, and at the end of the year diplomas presented.

The fire of 1870 destroyed all the property so carefully accumulated during the first years of the society's existence. Left once more without library or furnishings, its members held their meetings for a time at Centenary Church. Sigma Pi, ever gallant in time of need, offered the use of its library. But before 1874 Phi Nu must have returned to the building, for it is recorded that the society, in that year, purchased a new piano, having previously been obliged to adjourn to the social room for the musical part of its program.

In 1875, at a joint Exhibition of Phi Nu and Belles Lettres, the members of the former society each wore on her left shoulder a tin badge with Phi Nu unmistakably inscribed upon it. The next year they appeared at a Belles Lettres open meeting with a gold ivy leaf worn with a white bow on the left shoulder. Since that time the pin has gone through two more stages of development, shrinking in size with each, having been an oak leaf before it assumed its present form of a a maple leaf. The Phi Nu color was originally yellow, but changed later to blue—an exact reversal of the process through which the Belles Lettres color had gone.

The iniation ceremony was revised in 1895. Apparently its previous form had not been sufficiently impressive, though it is related that one girl was so terrified she ran away during its operation.

Perhaps the custom of the early years that strikes as the most odd, was that of taking in men as honrary members. Occasionally the same man will appear several times on the roll, as having been voted in by different members. Among their number we find several men of note: Ex-Governor Oglesby, Honorable Schulyer Colfax, Mont Cranston of Denver, Colorado, Ex-Governor Palmer (and wife). Most of these men had, it seems, gained their popularity by presenting the society with books or pictures.

A large part of the history of Belles Lettres and Phi Nu is concerned with their struggle to obtain permanent halls of their own. Until 1914, they were permitted to give an annual play—usually considered the big event of the year—and to pocket the returns. It was with this money, chiefly, that they managed, at length, to purchase their halls. Meanwhile many years passed during which they had no definite meeting place. At first they scarcely had a corner in which to place their few volumes, and held their meetings in class rooms or in a section in the Old Chapel. But, in Dec. 1897, Belles Lettres moved into the Lurton house, standing where the library now stands (the Main Building ending at that time, with Mr. Metcalf's office), and the March of the following year Phi Nu moved into an upper room of the same house. We read in that year's "Greetings" that Belles Lettres hall was decorated in yellow and that it contained comfortable furniture and a number of book-cases. The Phi Nu report says contentedly: "Phi Nus are now permanently located in their new hall. The furnishings are all blue and white * * and the room is very dainty and beautiful and already seems to have quite a literary air about it."

But from almost the first minute of their entrance into the building the societies began to work for a new hall. The plays, candy-pulls and sales by which they had obtained money for their rooms in the Lurton building were strenuously received. Gifts came in from alumnae, special assessments were made on active members, and, at last, in 1902, they were able to move into their new halls—the two rooms, comprising the present library, which Dr. Harker had built for their express purpose. Phi Nu occupied the south room, Belles Lettres the north. By 1905 they had completely paid off their debt of $500 each.

But when plans for Harker Hall began to be formulated, the societies were busy again. In fact even before they had finished paying for their rooms in the Main building, we find their reports (from 1903-1909) full of aspirations for halls in the new building. More candy pulls, sales, entertainments, receiving of gifts, until in 1909, they moved triumphantly into the present society halls.

This goal achieved, there was, however, still sufficient incentive to work. New furnishings must be bought and the library increased, and finally, their share toward endowment raised. Fortunately, they retained their privilege of giving plays until all these things were accomplished. One would expect now to find them contentedly resting on their past achievements. But not so. Ambition o'erleaps itself, it seems, and bids fair to fall on the prosperous side. There is a plan afloat——which will be divulged in a page or two.

*　　　*　　　*　　　*

Membership in Belles Lettres and Phi Nu being limited, when the college grew to its present proportion there was a consequent need for new societies. In 1912 on the evening of Founder's Day, Miss Weaver, the dean, called twenty girls (mostly Freshmen) to her room for a private consultation. She explained to them this need for new societies and that Belles Lettres and Phi Nu had both generously agreed to invite to membership during that entire year, only sisters of their own members, thus giving the new society an open field for their start. She told these girls that they had been chosen as the founders because of their influence and ability and qualities of leadership. They could not fail to appreciate the honor and set to their task with the utmost enthusiasm. Next evening they met in Phi Nu Hall and Celia Cathcart, President of Phi Nu, and Emily Jayne Allan, President of Belles Lettres, told them something of what their responsibilities would be, and offered to help them in every way possible.

The girls were then divided into groups of ten each —an attempt being made to divide them acording to a balance of qualities—and thereafter the two groups met separately. One became Theta Sigma, the other, Lambda Alpha Mu. They held their meetings in secret for a time, while they drew up their constitution, decided on their pin, flower, and colors (Theta Sigma choosing the Kilarney rose for its flower and lavendar for its color; Lambda Alpha Mu choosing the chrysanthemum for its flower, black, gold and scarlet for its colors) and selected their society song. Madeline McDaniels' was selected for Theta Sigma and Ruth Want's for Lambda Alpha Mu. Theta Sigma's motto was: "From faith to virtue, from virtue to knowledge." Lamba Mu's "Let us strike a higher strain."

Dr. Harker set the day for the new societies to appear in chapel, and amid an awed silence they filed in and seated themselves in the two back rows. They all wore white dresses, the Theta Sigmas' decorated with black arm bands on which were their letters in red and yellow, the Lambdu Mus' wearing pink Kilarney roses and lavendar bows pined on with silver pledge pins.

Though news of the societies had leaked out before, nothing definite was known, and it was with a good deal of excitement that the assembled students listened to Dr. Harker's address and his introduction of the charter members of the new societies. They were: Ida Perry, Louise Frank, Maud Collins, Hazel Keblinger, Mary Shastid, Jane Culmer, Florence Haller, Mary Louise Powell, and Ruth Want, founders of Lambda Mu and Mary Baldridge, Marie Johnson, Mabel Larson, Honore Limerick, Irene Merrill, Helen McGhee, Grace Roberts, Mildred Seaman, Geneva Upp, and Lucile White,—founders of Theta Sigma.

At first these societies like their predecessors, had no home. They met in the old chapel and in Expression Hall until, in their second year, they were offered the rooms above the Y. W. C. A. room in Harker Hall, Lambda Alpha Mu now occupying the one on the fourth floor, Theta Sigma the one on the fifth. These rooms were of course very small and proved inadequate for their they were given their present rooms in the main building.

Started as they were under the most favorable auspices possible, the Dean and the President not only requesting their existence, but doing everything in their power to encourage their growth, and the older societies postponing their rivalry for a whole year, lending in the meantime the friendliest kind of a helping hand, Theta Sigma and Lambda Alpha Mu have already reached the point where there is nothing to choose between them and the older societies.

A committee on inter-society relationships has recently been formed to encourage the mutual understanding among the societies, and it is hoped that, in spite of the natural rivalry among organizations whose growth and alertness is consequent largely upon just such rivalry, there will develop a spirit of essential sisterhood—a sisterhood based upon common interests, common aims, and, if rumor has it rightly, even a common dwelling place! There is word abroad that these four societies desire a house quite by themselves, where they may have rooms for meetings and a banquet hall, be in short, lords of their own domain. If achievement in the past is any indication of achievement in the future, the gymnasium will not be the only building to make its appearance on the campus in the next few years. —Dorothea Washburne.

Y. W. C. A.

To the students of 1916 the Y. W. C. A. is such a vital organization that we can scarcely think of a time when it did not exist. Yet there was a time, and that not so very long ago, when there was no organized Christian Association. Almost from the beginning of the college there had been a kind of organization that was sometimes called an Epworth League. This was important, for it was the nucleus of our Y. W. C. A. The college grew in numbers and with this growth came the feeling of the lack of a student organization that would be a meeting ground for all girls. Definite steps were taken, and in November, 1899, with the help of the lady principal, Miss Austin, and the interest of other faculty members the little nucleus was organized into a Young Woman's Christian Association consisting of twenty-five members. In the first cabinet were Leah McIvane, president, Josephine Wright, vicepresident, Lura Chaffee, treasurer, Mable Helem, secretary. The history of the Y. W. C. A. for the next year or two is not all that we might hope for it to be. After the first enthusiasm of a new organization, interest languished; and it was the help and zeal of the faculty that kept the organization going. However by 1902 the Y. W. C. A. had passed its initiative state; the membership increased to one hundred and the first representative; Amy Fackt, was sent to the Geneva Conference. From this time on we find in almost every number of the Greetings a report of its works and activity.

It was about this time, too, that the association first had a home. It could hardly be called room, for it was only a space curtained off on the east alcove of the second floor, main; nevertheless it was a place where the cabinet could hold its meetings and where the girls could "drop in" and have a good time. After the completion of Harker Hall the room on the third floor was given to the Association, and this is still our home.

Just a word about some of the customs of the Y. W. C. A. For sixteen years the Freshmen has been helped in her adjustment to college life; Y. W. girls have met her at the train, assisted her in registration and in many other ways aided her in those first days of homesickness. then, since its very beginning, the party for the new girls on the first Saturday night has been an annual event of the Y. W. C. A. The first May breakfast, the spring frolic we look forward to with so much anticipation, was given on May 8, 1905. There has always been a bazaar just before the Christmas vacation; true, in the olden days it was designated by the word "sale", but with the change in other lines has come a change in this, and we now call it our Christmas bazaar.

The Y. W. C. A. has become a part of the college,

and, as the college grows, so the Y. W. C. A. will grow. We can say in 1916, as the Jubilee writer said in 1904, "As the future of a few years ago is the present of to-day, so to-day also has its future." For truly the Young Woman's Christian Association is the one meeting ground for all girls; it is here they gather for the one common purpose of helping each other to a brighter vision of life and its possibilities.

—Ruth Mendenhall.

ATHLETICS.

Work — fun — basket ball — tennis — dreams the high school graduate as she packs her trunk in the fall for college. She is justified in her dreams too, for athletics enter vitally into student life everywhere. The Illinois Woman's College has not differed from other schools in this respect.

In March, 1894, a beautiful banner of heliotrope satin and velvet with I. F. C. and a pair of dumb-bells worked on it was presented to the Athletic Association. This banner became the inspiration of many a hard fought struggle in the following years.

The first field meet at the Woman's College occurred in 1900. As we read about it in the College Greetings we hold our breath until we learn that the freshman-junior team won the basket ball game, and the senior-sophomore representatives, the tennis contest.

Year by year the college athletics grew. Basket ball games between the Brownies and the Midgets, Princton and Cornell, Yale and Harvard, took place in the gymnasium. Tennis was so popular that seven courts were kept busy.

With this interest in athletics the natural desire of the student body was a new gymnasium. Accordingly a definite campaign to earn money for a building was started. Plays and circuses produced by the Athletic Association were enjoyed by the whole school, while the proceeds were added to the growing gymnasium fund. Some friend of the college promised to duplicate every dollar raised in a given time by the students. In 1906 one thousand dollars was handed to Dr. Harker to be used in the erection of a gymnasium. Although circumstances made it necessary to postpone the building of a gymnasium at that time, when our dream is fulfilled, as we feel it soon will be, these former students of the college will know that they have had a big share in it.

For a few years interest in things athletic declined. In the spring of 1913, however, a new spirit was manifested. The hike club organized, then went along with vim until their contests closed. That same year, the faculty presented the Athletic Association with a beautiful loving cup, on which were to be inscribed the names of the winners of the tennis tournament. This gift probably was the incentive which brought about the building of the new hard tennis court. The joy over the cup was only equalled by that over a silver and mahogany shield on which are engraved the names of the victorious basket ball teams.

Toward the end of each school year comes the track meet. Girls appear in bloomers and middies throughout the day. We hear rumors of a "Training table" and a "Good night's sleep." It is strange with what excellent grace sore muscles and aching bones are endured in order to win the much contested association pin.

The Athletic Association feels that it stands on firm ground. It believes that the need is not so much for a greater variety of sports, as it is for an even greater interest in the ones which we now have. Visions come of rousing hockey games and of keen competition in base ball.

Of course all these sports take time, but we can almost hear the old girls say, "Take time? Indeed they do, but they are worth it. Keep your spirits up."

Then, students of the Illinois College, let us make the new girl's dream come true.

—May Blackburn, '16·

OUR LIBRARY

A few collections of books and a few magazines housed in what is now the English recitation room, constituted the college library for many years. As time passed we awakened suddenly to the fact that this department was not keeping pace with the phenomenal growth of the College along other lines.

When Harker Hall was completed the few thousand volumes were moved to the west wing of the main building and placed in modern stacks. With new tables, a better light and various other improvements, we felt that at least we had the beginning of a real library.

Those who were here during the winter and spring of 1910-11 will never forget our campaign for a greater library culminating in what was known as "Library Day," April 12, 1911. In books and money the result of our labor amounted to $1,246.00. This was the forerunner of still greater activity to increase the library facilities.

The College Guild, our next friend, through two years of effort, added several hundred more books, enriching the various departments to an appreciable extent; nor have we despised the smaller gifts from friends, both in Jacksonville and throughout the state, who have remembered the Library from time to time. With this recent gift of one thousand volumes, we have felt that like Longfellow's Turnip, we had grown and grown until we could grow no longer, (at least in our present quarters), When Lo, a modern prophet arises, who says to us—"Enlarge the place of thy tent, and let them stretch forth the curtains of thine habitations," and behold, I will pay the bill."

THE SPECTATOR AGAIN.

In accordance with a certain foolish habit, the Spectator decided to make one of his periodic visits to the College, to learn what the young ladies did with their spare time. He supposed that he would find them either diligently studying, or quietly knitting for deserving Belgians, but even the briefest of visits dispelled his old fashioned ideas. Like all the rest of their busy sisters, he found the college girls to be Club mad. No sooner had he closed the front door than he heard one girl say to her companion, "Say, Lou, where are we going at 4:15?" The other answered, "Why, I've got to go to Dramatic club practice, but I'm going to beat it as soon as I can, because the Indiana club wants to plan a stunt for Saturday night. And if I get through these in time enough for dinner I want to go to that French Club committee meeting. Why, what did you want to know for?"

Oh! nothing special, I just thought if you weren't busy I'd get you to help me get my demonstration for the Home Economic's Club ready, and then we'd go get some hambergers. This is roast beef night! "Oh, I'm sorry, but honest I don't see how I can."

They passed out of hearing and the Spectator shook his head, puzzled not only over the many "gets", but sadly confused by such a number of interests as seemed to attract the student's attention. Seeking for some one who was not so entangled in activities, consumed the better part of an hour, and then his informant kept one eye on her wrist watch to be sure she wouldn't miss her Madrigal Club practice. No longer, it seemed, did the literary societies furnish sufficient diversion, and just as Mr. Business Man demands a cabaret with his dinner so does Miss College Girl demands clubs and clubs and still more clubs to help her, "throw aside the rigors of her regular work, his informant had said. In his hand he held a list of these organizations and the Madrigal Club practice was the only reason it wasn't longer. The first was the German Club, to help us to be more interested in our regular German courses you know; the girl had told him. The Spectator thought this wasn't such a bad idea. In fact for it and "LeCircle Francais" he felt not a little sympathy. If only every girl in the school didn't want to be in each of them. Surely it would be confusing to talk intelligently one day about Goethe or Sudermann and the next day to as intelligently discuss Moliere or Brieux. The Spectator sighed as he thought of the leisurely manner in which he had made friends of these notables, and recalled how the girl had laughed and said, "Yes Faust is kind of deep, but then you can look interested and ask high brow questions," and as for Moliere, ' Pshaw, when I want to laugh, I read "Life.'"

What attractions it does take to make girls believe they're studying, thought the Spectator as he read the next name "Glee Club." Perhaps it was lonesome to practice alone in a room just big enough for a piano and one. He had never found it so, but then he was "queer" anyway. He liked old ways and old things but nowadays "change" is the slogan. Even the name had "gone stale", that up-to-date young person had said so they changed it to "Madrigal Club", and she had further added, "You know it does so promote college spirit for the sixteen or seventeen of us to get to-gether and practice and interchange ideas."

Interchange ideas! The Spectator was lost in wondering when they had time to acquire those ideas and then his eye fell on the next name and he read, Home Economics Club. Even the newer departments had taken up with this strange order of things. He smiled a little as he recalled the special merits of this one, "The May meeting is always great, we always have a dandy picnic, you know." Being only a Spectator he did not venture the opinion that thanks to classes, societies and general friendliness picnics were not a rarity, and anyway the girl had continued, "We really get a lot out of it, you know, for we do keep in touch with what outsiders are doing along the lines of Home Economics." Outsiders he was left to conclude might be those of the laity who made fudge in the corridors or perhaps they might be the devotees of Mrs. Rorer. She hadn't had time to tell him that.

There was one more name on his list, "Dramatic Club." Did the three hundred aspire to be Mary Pickfords or Julia Marlowes? Indigantly he had been told that the membership was limited to those already possessing ability equal to or excelling that of those public favorites. Not only was the best dramatic talent thus trained and developed, but the purpose of the club was wholly altruistic. They gave plays and for these plays they sold tickets. The money, she proudly told him, was given to the college for the endowment fund.

As the Spectator crossed off this last organization he smiled, they were so earnest, these children, playing with grown-ups toys, clubs and associations. Had he missed something because he had played long the role of spectator rather than that of participator? If he were young again would he, too, be rushing to meetings with youthful enthusiasm? He was no longer smiling as he pondered.

Z. M.—"Greek tragedy arose from religious origin."

K. B.—"Gladiators were slaves, criminals, Christians, etc."

L. C.—"Peaple who had charge of the races were called, factories."

A Special—Miss A. "I always hate to get 'Special Delivery Letters. I'm afraid to open them."

A. F.—"Oh! I like to get 'Specials' I always know what't in them."

M. H.—Did you hear what that man said to the lady?

F. M.—Where's a man?

M. H.—Well! Have you gone to I. W. C., so long you don't
know the species?

G. W.—"What part in the play does Corinne have?"
P. W.—"She is Hero."
L. S.—"Well, then, who's going to be the heroine?"

L. C.—"The Arena of the amphitheater was epileptic in shape."

M. J.—"Were you ever told not to eat the hole in the doughnut?"

M. O.—"Yes, indeed! I never do. It's bad for you."

T. C.—(innocently) "I never do either, for I don't like them."

INGRATITUDE

Indignant Sophomore—"And she asked me if I thought she was any father, and because she was a visitor and only here for a few days I thought I'd be polite and say no, she laughed right thin! and she went off right away to Margaret and said I get father every time I take a breath!"

K. B. Going down stairs on crutches.

G. M.—Oh what's the matter have you broken your foot?

G. W.—"Have you ever been to a Turkey Run?"

L. S.—"No, but I've been at an egg rolling."

H. D.—"What was that funny joks someone told at our table last night? I tried to tell it and found that I had forgotten."

Table, excitedly, "What was it about?"

H. D.—"I can't remember!"

M. B. "Edna has never seen cotton growing. Isn't that funny?"

E. R. "Mary has never seen a corn crib. Isn't that funny?"

M. B. "Down at Helen's they get their water from a pump instead of a faucet. Isn't that funny?"

From Caesar test—"The walls were striped of defenders."
E. P.—"awribus teneo lupum—I hold the wolf with gold."

| Music Hall | Main Building | Extension | Harker Hall |
| Erected 1906 | Erected 1850 | Erected 1902 | Erected 1909 |

ILLINOIS WOMAN'S COLLEGE

College of Liberal Arts
College of Music
School of Fine Arts
School of Expression
School of Home Economics
A Standard College

Regular college and academy courses leading to Bachelor's degree. Pre-eminently a Christian college with every facility for thorough work. Located in the Middle West, in a beautiful, dignified, old college town, noted for its literary and music atmosphere.

Let us have names of your friends who are looking for a good college.

Call or address, Registrar,

ILLINOIS WOMAN'S COLLEGE

Jacksonville, Illinois

"All golden the years that shall crown thee with light......
    Yet farther and more shalt thou seek,
Though far reaching aeons which beckon thee on
    The Voice of the future shall speak.

Alma mater, beloved, it shall ever be thine,
    To widen the boundary of youth
To wing the young spirit with strength for its flight,
    In the domain of knowledge and truth.

                    —Martha Capps Oliver.

Lightning Source UK Ltd.
Milton Keynes UK
UKHW052035191218
334046UK00008BA/755/P